from Within

by Karen B. Hall

Copyright © 2015 Karen B. Hall

All rights reserved.

DEDICATION

"MOTHER"

Betty McDow Rushing passed away Friday, January 4th, 2008, at Jeffrey Place Healthcare and Rehabilitation Center in Waco, Texas.

Betty was born December 5,1939 at Honey Grove, Texas to James Luther McDow, Sr. and Josephine Ivodel-McDow. She was one of nine brothers and sisters including a twin sister. The family did not have much money; however they had each other and God. My grandfather died one year before I was born.

Later in life my mom at the age of sixteen married a man name David E. Rushing. What is ironic my dad did not see me for the first year I was born. He was in the army and he died one year before my daughter was born. I will tell more about my dad in later chapters.

God put this message on my heart to tell you about how Jesus Loves You whatever circumstances you are facing and that there is hope, healing, and salvation. I pray that you accept Jesus unconditional love and accept Jesus as your savior and be healed growing in faith and love.

Isaiah 61:1 (NIV version)

The spirit of the Lord God is upon me because the Lord has anointed me to bring good news in the suffering and afflicted. He has sent me in comfort the brokenhearted.

CONTENTS

	Acknowledgments	i
	Introduction	1
1	Depression	3
2	Generational Curse	7
3	Fear	11
4	Anxiety and Worry	17
5	Trauma	21
6	Addiction	27
7	Low Self-Esteem	31
8	Control	35
9	Approval Addiction	39
10	Physical Conditions	43
11	Guilt and Condemnation	47
12	Words	51
13	Let's Pray	55
	Conclusion	59
	Journal	61
	About the Author	75

ACKNOWLEDGMENTS

THANK YOU TO ALL MY FAMILY AND FRIENDS FOR YOUR SUPPORT AND LOVE. THE MOST IMPORTANT IS A THANK YOU TO JESUS CHRIST FOR PUTTING THESE WORDS ON MY HEART AND YOUR WILL BE DONE ON EARTH AS IT IS IN HEAVEN. A SPECIAL THANK YOU TO PASTORS STEVE AND SHARON KELLY FOR ALL YOUR BIBLICAL TEACHINGS, OUR PASTORS STEVE AND CYNDI ABBE WHO WE HAVE COME TO KNOW AND LOVE AND THANK YOU FOR YOUR BIBLICAL TEACHINGS. A SPECIAL THANKS TO MY MOM AND DAD FOR HAVING US AND BEING THE BEST THEY COULD BE, MY CHILDREN EVAN, ASHLI AND KOBY, GOD MADE ME STRONGER THROUGH MY CIRCUMSTANCES TO BE THE BEST MOM I COULD BE AND THANK YOU FOR YOUR LOVE AND SUPPORT. A SPECIAL THANK YOU TO KIM RICHTER WHO IS MY BEST FRIEND AND LIKE A SISTER TO ME. A SPECIAL THANKS GRANDMA FOR YOUR STRENGHTH AND GUIDANCE I WILL SEE YOU SOON. AND MOST OF ALL THANK YOU THE LOVE OF MY LIFE KEN HALL. GOD BLESS YOU!

LOVE YOU ALL!

JUST A NOTE:

As you read through this book, use the journal pages to write down your thoughts and feelings.

Be still and listen to what God is trying to say to you.

INTRODUCTION

What I remember about my mom is when my sister Lisa and I waking up on a Sunday morning and mom is taking rollers out of our hair and dressing us in frilly, lacy dresses for church.

I'm frantically brushing the curls out of my hair, being the tomboy that I was when mom was not looking. I remember my mom taking us to Church and me asking why do we have to go to Church and not being very enthusiastic about going.

I now thank you, Mom, for taking us to Church and for teaching us good morals in life and how life should be lived. Thank you for having Lisa and myself and being there for us.

After every conversation instead of saying "Goodbye" you always ended the conversation with "God Bless You!"

We don't understand why you had to go through the pain and suffering you did and it wasn't meant for us to understand. I know God had a plan and a purpose for your life and I truly believe you carried out that plan, even though you were sick most of your life.

Part of that plan was to be a caregiver for the kids at church and for moms and dads who worked outside the home so they could provide for their families and for having Lisa and me.

Now, Mom, you are home with Jesus and with your teachings Lisa and I are going to carry out God's plan for our lives. We shed tears for you departing, however we know you are in no more pain, and with Jesus you have a smile back on your face and back to having that beautiful smooth skin that you once had. We will see you one day soon again.

WE LOVE YOU!

1
DEPRESSION

There are all types of depression. Most people with depression need medical attention. I believe God put people on this earth to treat illnesses and one of these illnesses is depression, however I want to encourage you to take on another view point and consider giving it all to God. I will explain in later chapters how you can do this.

Some of the different types of depression I am going to talk about are what I experienced within me or family and close friends that were around me. Mom and dad were one of these family members.

I might not have all the answers, but I do know one thing – that out of my experience with depression, God was on my side and totally freed me up from these terrible feelings. He made me a stronger person. Depression can lead to alcohol, drugs to name a couple that I turned to when hurting.

I was determined not to depend on alcohol, drugs, or even prescription medications. I became tired of trying to heal myself. I refused to go to doctors or clinics to get over the counter medication just because I have seen what my mom went through with her medications. I am not telling you not go to the doctors or get on medications, this was my choice. People do have choices in the power of Jesus and I choose to totally depend on Jesus to solve my problems.

This is what I want to share with you.

I hope and pray dear Father God this will help people to become free and happy and to live life to the fullest. Dear Father God I put all my trust in you and your power once people accept Jesus as there Savior that there will be miracles of healing performed and wipe out depression and addictions in Jesus Christ name I pray. AMEN!

So as we go forward keep an open mind and focus not on your emotions but focus on the Jesus I am about to share with you.

I hate depression, addiction and willing to share because I am obedient to God and because I love you!

Here is a list of some of the symptoms of depression:

1. Constant feelings of sadness, irritability or tension.

2. Decreased interest or pleasure in usual activities or hobbies.

3. Loss of energy, feeling tired despite lack of activity.

4. A change in appetite, with significant weight loss

or weight gain.

5. A change in sleeping patterns, such as difficulty sleeping or sleeping too much.

6. Restlessness or feeling slowed down.

7. Decreased ability of making decisions or concentrate.

8. Feelings of worthlessness, hopelessness or guilt.

9. Thoughts of suicide and death.

Journal

Date: _____

2
GENERATIONAL CURSE

All my life I have been around people with depression and/or addiction. Depression can be family history. According to medical society genetics play a role in depression and can run in families for generation after generation.

NEWS FLASH

I come from a family with history of depression and have been told according to medical viewpoint that I will have depression. Both my mom and dad became schizophrenic. The reason my parents had this illness is beyond my understanding and I know it is not meant for me to understand so I put my trust in God.

I was determined not to carry on this generational curse by putting Jesus in my life and learning how to trust, obey, and be teachable. It did not come fast we just can't give up and keep moving forward. The power of Jesus with faith, hope, and trust can move in your life with awesome and amazing directions. Jesus is your best friend, daddy, provider, healer, and savior.

This is my encouragement to you is accept Jesus as your Savior. With faith let's put an end to what your circumstance is and move forward.

Dear Father God, people through generations had illnesses with depression and addictions. I pray and command this curse with the power of Jesus be broken and I pray people will come to know you and be teachable and learn how to increase faith and trust. IN JESUS NAME I PRAY! AMEN!

I realized that being depressed is not fair to my husband and kids and we do not want to carry on this disease to members of our families. So let's keep moving and it's OK to cry out to Jesus to help us. I cried out many nights for Jesus to help break this disease and addictions.

Psalms 34: 4,15 (NIV version)

I sought the Lord, and he heard me, and delivered me from all my fears ... The eyes of the Lord are on the righteous and His ears are open to their cry.

Lord I am asking you to listen to your children's cry and deliver them from their illness and addictions.

> POWER OF JESUS YOU CAN BREAK THIS GENERATIONAL CURSE!

Journal
Date: _____

Journal

Date: _____

3
FEAR

Fear is attack from Satan. He wants destruction and devastation. Fear can stop us from experiencing life, peace, and joy. The life that God wants us to have is peace and joy.

"LION HEART"

In the year 1911 King Richard the Lion Heart was a Christian crusader who fought against the Muslims and fighting for Jerusalem with Muslims trying to take over Jerusalem. King Richard did win many battles slaughtering thousands of Muslims convinced this was God's will.

The Muslims believed they had the true cross and the Muslim leader Salazar, hearing of this, was furious and this started a holy war over Jerusalem.

Both came together in battle. The Muslims fled and Salado defeated, however the Muslim troops still captured some Christian crusaders and beheaded them.

As winter rolled around King Richard headed for Jerusalem. The troops traveled by horses and foot. Many people died from exposure and weather conditions worsened. King Richard ordered the troops to turn back and return home. Many of the men in disgust did not want to turn back, but wanted to travel on, and they looked upon King Richard as a coward.

King Richard returned to England to fight for his crown and fell into a deep depression and came to realize he never should have abandoned Jerusalem. King Richard, with the weather improving and his reputation at stake, again journeyed to Jerusalem.

For the second time King Richard came so close outside of Jerusalem setting up camp, being able to see men inside the city swelled with fear and turned away from battle and again returned heading home.

The third time he went out again on a journey to Jerusalem not making it went into battle of Jaff winning his reputation back, however he became sick of exhaustion and died never making it to Jerusalem.

King Richard had the fear of failure. My motto is JUST DO IT! Don't let fear swallow you up. Push forward and go for it.

Psalms 112: 7-8 (GNT)

I am not afraid of receiving bad news; my faith is strong, and I trust in the Lord, I am not worried or afraid.

Proverbs 29:25 (NIV)

The fear of man brings a snare, but because I lean on, trust in, and put my confidence in the Lord, I am safe and set on high.

Psalm 23:4 (NIV)

Yes, though I walk through valley of the shadow of death, I will fear or dread no evil, for you are with me; your rod (to protect) and Your Staff (to guide), they comfort me.

Let's see another history story. This is about King David.

"DAVID DEFEATS GOLIATH"

Goliath a Philistine started walking toward David, with his shield bearer walking in front of him. Coming closer and getting a good look at David, he was filled with scorn for him. Challenging David and calling down curses, with his sword, spear and javelin. David comes against Goliath in the name of the Lord, putting this giant in the power of David who trust in the Lord and with no fear defeated the giant. The Lord does not need swords, spears to save his people. He is victorious in battle, and he will put all of you in his power. David with only a stone and slingshot slung at Goliath and hit him in the forehead and broke his skull and Goliath lying face down on the ground and so without a sword, David defeated and killed Goliath with only a sling and a stone. David took Goliath's sword, cutting off his head and killed him. David started out as a boy watching over sheep and God increased him to being a King, David continued with many other battles and trials and him as well at one time depressed after displeasing God with Bathsheba he pressed forward.

JUST DO IT!

Journal

Date: _____

_____
_____
_____
_____
_____
_____
_____
_____
_____
_____
_____
_____
_____
_____
_____
_____
_____
_____
_____

Journal

Date: _____

4
ANXIETY AND WORRY

Have you ever woken up in the middle of the night worrying about something we can't do anything about at that moment? Most of the time situations that arise are out of our hands and control.

Anxieties and worries can lead to depression. Worries are thoughts that go through your mind over and over and over again and this is an insecurity and attack from Satan. The devil loves to hone in on our thoughts and insecurities and when we do this more negativity starts entering our minds. This is not God.

Matthew 6: 31, 33 (NKJV version)

Therefore do not worry about tomorrow, for tomorrow will worry about its own things. Sufficient for the day is its own trouble.

Therefore do not worry about tomorrow, for tomorrow will worry about its own things. (Plain and simple enough for me).

I used to wake up in the middle of the night and start thinking and worrying about the bills, work, looking at the clock every five minutes. Now when I wake up at night I start singing praises or praying.

Worry can lead to anxiety and anxiety can lead to panic attacks.

"GOING INTO BATTLE"

Put all your worries and anxieties in God's hands and not put too much on yourself.

In later chapters I am going to share some memories of the past (which is not easy but gave me strength). I will not let fear overtake me.

Dwelling on the past is another weapon that Satan uses to put in your head so you begin to have anxieties and worries that can lead to depression and feel you're not good enough.

The reason I am going to share my past with you is to give you a sense of understanding about God's work in my life and show how that if God can work in my life he can work in your life. Allow God to work in your life and delete depression and accept God's love. Sometimes God also allows circumstances to happen in your life and use you as a testimony to help others. I feel that is what God is doing with me.

Journal

Date: _____

Journal

Date: _____

5
TRAUMA

Depression can be caused by trauma that had happened or is happening in your life, such as divorce, death of a love one, financial problems, disease, and family disturbance to name a few.

I have been surrounded by people going through one of these situations that I have mentioned including myself. It could be in your past or present.

Psalm 42:5 (NIV version)

Why are you downcast O my soul? Why so disturbed within me? Put your hope in God, for I will yet praise him, my savior and my God.

Psalm 42:5 (NKJV version)

Why are you cast down, O my soul? And why are you disquieted within me? Hope in God, for I shall yet praise Him for the help of His countenance.

"MY CHILDHOOD"

In my childhood I faced some challenging times such as abuse, alcoholism, and drugs. I was baptized at age of twelve then HELL broke loose! This is not easy for me to share, however by the will of God I pray my testimony will help you. I want to give you good news that what happened in the past or even your present that you can be delivered and strengthened by the grace and mercy of God.

"DAD"

I was born when my dad was in the Army and did not see me until I was one year old. My dad as a child accepted Christ and was baptized at the age of twelve. My dad married my mom at age of twenty. I remember as a child dad and I being close. I was his tomboy. He taught me how to change a tire on the car, change the oil on the car, rake leaves, chop wood and the most memorable time was building a raft to go down the creek. Our favorite games were horse shoes, washers, and badminton. As I grew older I noticed changes in my dad that I do not understand and am probably not meant to understand. He started becoming isolated, controlling, jealous, yelling at us all the time (cussing), and abusive (mentally and physically). He was seeing ghosts, hearing voices, and locking us in the house because he thought neighbors were coming after us. He was schizophrenic. We became afraid of dad. Dad went home to Jesus at the age of 46 with an aneurysm of the brain. I question what caused his illness – was it the aneurysm, army or medications?

"MOM"

Mom always the one taking us to church, being a

caregiver to the nursery children, and for families that worked outside the home she took care of their children. After caring for kids and the family, our mother became weak in strength and the problems from dad just escalated. At the age thirteen I remember standing in the kitchen and she told me if your dad did not change he is going to drive me crazy. I, at a tender age, telling her to get a divorce not really knowing what that meant, and she said that was not in her vocabulary and that generation did not believe in divorces.

Mom had a nervous breakdown. Dad became more controlling, jealous, and isolated. Mom got addicted to her prescriptions causing her two more nervous breakdowns. She too became schizophrenia hearing voices. She ended up in a nursing home with her mind diminishing. The last time I visited my mom she did not know me. The one thing that always on my mind is that she remembered one thing and that was the words to "Amazing Grace" and she sang them beautifully. I lost my mom January 4, 2008.

"GRANDMOTHER"

My hero! As a teenager it was a difficult time, raising ourselves at times. One person I do look up too and admire and who I love so much was my grandmother (My dad's mom). She was a strong and courageous woman. The stories and journey in her life was amazing. She stepped in with love, kindness, forgiveness to help us and love my sister and I. I went with her for grocery shopping, and became close. She, too, was baptized at young age and close to Jesus. She died at the age of ninety nine years old, two weeks from her one hundredth birthday. Her birthday August 3, 2013, she died in July 2013. One story she told was when she went through a depression. She, too, had the strength to fight from within. Grandma, I Miss You and love You! MY HERO!

Psalms 18:2-3 (NIV version)

The Lord is my rock and my fortress and my deliverer, my strength, in whom I will trust: My shield and the horn of my salvation, my stronghold. I will call Upon the Lord, who is worthy to be praised: So shall I be saved from my enemies.

> FIGHT FROM WITHIN WHATEVER THE CIRCUMSTANCE!

Journal

Date: _____

Journal

Date: _____

6
ADDICTION

I want to introduce my family that God has blessed me with. I have wonderful husband named Ken. I met him at fifteen years old and we been together ever since. I married him when I was eighteen. I told you in the last chapter my grandmother was my hero, I leaned on Ken as well. When we first met and even into the beginning of our marriage we were known to be party animals as per say. The drinking and those funny little cigarettes came into our lives. We did the club scene and parties at the lake listening to "Pink Floyd" and other famous bands in that era known as classic rock. We did have bad times and the good times. My kids would agree that the good times were the best and that is when we put God on the top of our list and the head of our household. We have three beautiful kids (two sons and a daughter) and four grandchildren {two granddaughters and two grand boys}.

"MY BEAUTIFUL BABY GIRL"

Another major storm came! After my oldest son left home for the Navy we decided to move to Colorado from Texas. This is where my daughter had challenges. At the high school level she decided to drop out of school and follow a crowd that was involved in drugs. This drug that these kids were on was called methamphetamine. She was hooked.

At the same time I was pregnant with our third child who is now twelve and going on an amazing journey. At the time we were going to New Life Church and my faith in Jesus was maturing and growing strong. I refused to give up on my daughter. Understand we had police out at our house with our daughter being out of control, we had neighbors judging us, but one thing I kept focused on was Jesus. Prayer worked! MIRACLE!

One night my daughter called me weeping. At this point in her life she was thin, not eating, no money, unhealthy looking. I took my daughter to New Life for prayer. New Life had these prayer rooms you can go too to pray just for people who is together. It is a room where you and God can be alone. We read scriptures and prayed and just talked. Her addiction did not go right away, there were still struggles and challenges, but we kept the faith. Kicking her out of the house was not the solution. The answer was not giving up on her and fighting the good fight of faith.

I did go through a tough love course that gave me insight on some other methods on handling a child addicted to drugs. The economy at the time was not good in Colorado so I was laid off work. My oldest son suggested we move to Virginia so I can land a job and move forward. That is what I did. I took a three day bus trip to Virginia with my new born son and landed a job, three months later my husband came with my daughter. Did I give up on her NO! That was the tough love called unconditional love! That is what Jesus has for his children.

"UNCONDITIONAL LOVE"

One month later she went back to Colorado and brought her now husband back and he too off drugs. My daughter and I are best friends to this day and we would do whatever it takes for our family. I LOVE YOU MY BEAUTIFUL BABY GIRL! You are amazing wife and mother. Love, MOM!

"FRIENDS"

I have seen many friends with addictions commit suicide hooked on drugs and alcohol including myself at one time. One of my best friends hooked on drugs and alcohol that I love and never gave up on her. She always said she will never live past forty. They found her one morning dead three days before her forty year old birthday. The cause of death was accidental suicide. I know deep down in my heart she is with Jesus .We had our children close together and went on vacations and yes we partied together. She was like a sister to me. We had good conversations about Jesus as well. I LOVE YOU MY FRIEND! WILL SEE YOU SOON!

DON'T GIVE UP!

Journal

Date: _____

7
LOW SELF-ESTEEM

This is a subject I can relate to. From my experiences in my past I did develop a low self-esteem. I was chasing alcohol to drown my pain. I was shy and quiet. I was withdrawn from most people. It was hard for me to say no. Have you had people tell you that your dumb, skinny, fat, and feel hopelessness and worthless. DON'T! I always felt I was my dad's boy not his little princess.

"CHANGE"

What happen that changed me? I started hanging around positive people, listening to positive people, reading positive books, thinking positive thoughts. You've heard the phrase "If you can't help yourself you can't help others"! In my opinion that is not always true. I feel if you help others you are helping yourself. Don't always focus on just-yourself. Don't hang your head and not smile. Always smile and hold your head high. GOD LOVES YOU! You are his child. God has big plans for you. Be proud of whom you are no matter what your past or present circumstances are. Jesus will help you work it out, just start your journey with God.

"WHERE TO START"

1. Get planted in a bible teaching church.
2. Start reading God's word (start with one verse per day).
3. Pray (talk to God like I am talking to you).
4. Be a student of God's word.
5. Be childlike (God is your daddy).
6. Get around positive people.
7. Plug in and listen to positive people (CD's, DVD's, and Books).
8. When you make a mistake don't be so hard on yourself, give it to God.
9. Don't give up!

Some of role models to listen too!

1. Joyce Meyer
2. Steve and Sharon Kelly (Wave Church)
3. Steve and Cyndi Abbe (Crossroads)
4. Joel Olsten

HOLD YOUR HEAD HIGH!

Journal

Date: _____

Journal

Date: _____

8
CONTROL

Control and low self-esteem go hand in hand. When someone is constantly throwing out negativity (this is mental abuse) people start to believe them, especially children that grew up in this type of environment. Control is when someone is constantly telling you what you can and cannot do, and you don't have any independence or think for yourself. You also tend to start wanting to please people. You want to become a "GOD PLEASER" not a "PEOPLE PLEASER". Do not let people control your emotions and thoughts.

Galatians 1:10 (NKJV version)

For do I now persuade men or God? Or do I seek to please men? For if I still pleased men I would not be a bond servant of Christ.

Colossians 1:10 (NKJV version)

That you may walk, worthy of the Lord, fully pleasing Him, being fruitful in every good Work and increasing in the knowledge of God.

People in your life that try to control you have insecurities of their own and want to drag you down with them to make themselves feel better, even if they don't realize it. This can cause you as well have the same insecurities. Instead of trying to change these people, pray for these people and continue to focus on Jesus. People that are of this nature can be changed by our examples.

Thessalonians 2:4 (NKJV version)

But as we have been approved by God to be entrusted with the gospel, even so we speak not as pleasing men, but God who tests our heart.

The same way with husbands and wives. It does say submit to your husband and husbands love your wives as you do the church. We can't allow to be doormats for each other. In God's eyes we are to respect, be kind and love each other.

DON'T BE A DOORMAT!

Journal

Date: _____

Journal

Date: _____

_____
_____
_____
_____
_____
_____
_____
_____
_____
_____
_____
_____
_____
_____
_____
_____
_____
_____

9
APPROVAL ADDICTION

Last chapter I spoke to you about people pleasing. Part of people pleasing is approval from people. This is what I call approval addiction. Being raised in an environment of negativity made me search for people that will accept me. I was finding someone that will love me. I wanted people to like me.

People that are seeking approval from people will go to desperate measures and are not being themselves. These desperate measures are doing things with people that are not part of your lifestyle, such as drinking, drugs, agreeing with their opinions, dress how they dress, do what the world is doing. This is being a follower not a leader. Hollywood is a prime example of what "they think a person should be like" and sadly many people follow Hollywood profile. Not accepting who you are can cause other addictions.

These other addictions such as drug, alcohol, and eating disorders can lead to death. The one I do want to follow and be like is Jesus!

"Humility"

It was the will of the Lord that his servant grew like

a plant taking root in dry ground. He had no dignity or beauty to make us take notice of him. There was nothing attractive about him, nothing that would draw us to him. We despised him and rejected him, he endured suffering and pain. No one would even look at him – we ignored him as if he were nothing. But he endured suffering that should have been ours, the pain that we should have borne. All the while we thought that his suffering was punishment sent by God.

But because of our sins he was wounded, beaten, because of the evil we did. We are healed by the punishment he suffered, made whole by the blows he received. All of us were like sheep that were lost, each of us going his own way. But the Lord made the punishment fall on him, the punishment all of us deserved. He was treated harshly, but endured it humbly. Like a lamb about to be slaughtered, like a sheep about to be sheared, he never said a word. (Isaiah)

        BE YOURSELF WALKING IN THE SPIRIT!

Journal
Date: _____

_____
_____
_____
_____
_____
_____
_____
_____
_____
_____
_____
_____
_____
_____
_____
_____
_____
_____
_____

Journal

Date: _____

_____
_____
_____
_____
_____
_____
_____
_____
_____
_____
_____
_____
_____
_____
_____
_____
_____
_____
_____

10
PHYSICAL CONDITIONS

There are physical conditions that cause depression. They can be people that are dealing with cancer, HIV, heart disease to name a few.

My dad did have an aneurism on the brain. Did this cause his mental illness and depression and schizophrenia? This was put on my heart in later years when I was looking for answers about why my dad had this disease.

I remember my dad seeing visions of ghosts and hearing voices, constantly thinking people were after him and his family. Was it the brain aneurysm or was it trauma that may have occurred when he was in the Army? I will never know the real answer.

"HEALING"

There was a time in my life I dealt with possible cancer. After my oldest son left for the military we packed up and moved from Texas to Colorado. There my husband I were blessed with a new baby boy. (An "oops" baby!) He is the apple of our eye and I feel that God gave us another chance on raising another child. Shortly after my son was born I went in for a regular mammogram checkup and doctors found a lump in my left breast. Was I devastated you ask? YES! Did I get depressed? YES! I immediately put my focus on JESUS! The doctors set another appointment with intentions on how to remove this lump to see if it was malignant. One way was by needle. (Oh how I hate needles.) My relationship with Jesus was still growing and becoming stronger. I prayed dear Jesus to heal me. I would read, pray, stayed planted in church. My faith grew stronger and I put my total trust in him. My depression lifted. When I went to my next appointment they did another screening and THANK YOU JESUS! They could not find the lump. MIRACLE FROM GOD!

If you are dealing with a disease or illness I encourage you don't give up and keep focusing on Jesus. Read, pray, keep going to church if all possible. Have other people pray for you. The power of prayer is strong. Jesus still performs miracles today. I have seen it many of times in my life. He healed me from depression, drug use, alcoholism, and did away with the lump in my breast and ever since then when I go for a checkup I been cleared.

Dear Jesus, I pray for people that are facing diseases and illnesses that you lay your hand on their body and heal them. To know that you are with them and will never leave there side. I pray their faith be strengthened and there will trust in you. I pray you wipe out cancer, addictions, diabetes, and depression. I ask you to heal your children. Thank You for future healings and for loving us. IN JESUS' NAME I PRAY! AMEN.

Psalms 30:2 (NKJV version)

o Lord my God. I cried out to You, and You healed me.

Psalms 103: 2-4 (NKJV version)

Bless the Lord, O my soul, And forget not all His benefits: Who forgives all your iniquities (sins) Who heals all your diseases. Who redeems your life from Destruction. Who crowns you with lovingkindness and Tender mercies.

"FEAR" When faced with challenges due to health problems fear can set in. When I feel fear I again turn to Jesus. In an earlier chapter I said I would share some songs with you that I sing. Very simple songs. I start singing these and fear subsides. "Jesus Loves You" Jesus loves us this I know for the bible tells us so. Little ones to him belong they are weak but he is strong. Yes Jesus loves me! Yes Jesus loves me! Yes Jesus loves me for the bible tells us so. Another song is "Little Children of the World" Jesus loves the little children. All the children of the world, red, yellow, black and white Jesus loves the little children of the world. Jesus loves you, we are his children, give him a chance and ask Him for healing. The Power of Prayer works. Pray for the three "H's"

HEALING, HEALTH AND HAPPINESS!

Journal

Date: _____

11
GUILT AND CONDEMNATION

The enemy will try to make you and I feel guilty, even in the little things that happen in your life. When I make a mistake in my work or everyday life I will dwell on it for days. I tend to be hard on myself and put a lot of pressure on myself. God wants you to get over it.

When I was drinking heavily and smoking and going to the bars, when I came back to Christ guilt started pouring over me. Then God started working in my life. We are not perfect, only one man that walked on this earth is perfect and that is Jesus Christ our Savior.

When you accept Jesus as your Savior God forgets your past sins and that is why he sent his son Jesus to forgive us. He also sent you a gift (Holy Spirit, helper, consultant) that is inside you to help you.

"SEEK GOD"

You can seek God by reading his word, pray, go to church. He doesn't want you to feel guilt. Ask God to forgive you and accept his forgiveness.

Psalms 51: 1-2 (NKJV version)

Have mercy upon me 0 God. According to Your Loving kindness: According to the multitude of your tender mercies. Blot out my transgressions. Wash me thoroughly from my Iniquity. And cleanse me from my sin. God words goes on to say that He acknowledges your transgressions and our sins are a/ways before me. Against You. You only, have I sinned. And done this evil in your Sight-That You may be found just when you speak. And blameless when you judge.

So when you acknowledge your sins God will find you and when he judges, you're blameless.

Proverbs 15:15 (NKJV version)

All the days of the afflicted are evil. But he who is of a merry heart has a continual feast. Don't dwell on your past sins and your present sins ask God for forgiveness and the Holy Spirit will lead you to righteousness.

BE THE BEST YOU CAN BE!

Journal

Date: _____

Journal

Date: _____

12
WORDS

Words can be the most powerful in a person's life. Words are nouns, pronouns, verbs, etc.... Words are made up in sentences or statements. I am going to use statements. Words can be negative or words can be positive. Words can cause harm or words can protect. Do not use harmful words, but only helpful words, the kind that build you up and provide what is needed, so that is why you say helpful words so it will be good for those who hear you.

Words can cause mental abuse or words can uplift and encourage. Speak to one another with the words of psalms, hymns, and sacred songs; sing hymns and psalms to the Lord with praise in your hearts. Word can cause hurt feelings or words can cause happiness. Words can cause emotions. Emotion of love or hate.

The best word of all is LOVE. The worst word of all is HATE. Before you speak words listen. Always be in your right mind before you speak. Never speak words when you're angry, the word hate always comes out. Always speak when you're happy, the word love always comes. Jesus spoke in parables. This caused a person to think about his actions. Jesus never criticized, condemned or judged. The only time he used the word hate was for wickedness. He always used the word love for his children.

Since we are all God's dear children, you try to be like Jesus by having kindness, love, and respect in your heart. Let your life be controlled by love, just as Christ loves us. Do not let anyone deceive you with foolish words. Pick your friends wisely. Words can be spoken of truth or words can be spoken a lie. Words can be worthless or words can be valuable. Let your prayers not be made up of worthless words, but with authority and thanksgiving.

Last but not least WORDS that are spoken can cause a person to stay away from you or be drawn to you. It is your choice of words that are spoken.

        THE BEST WORD OF ALL IS LOVE!

Journal

Date: _____

_____
_____
_____
_____
_____
_____
_____
_____
_____
_____
_____
_____
_____
_____
_____
_____
_____

Journal

Date: _____

13
LET'S PRAY

If you have not accepted Jesus as your savior, I give you the opportunity to do so right now. I will pray with you. Dear Jesus, I ask you to come into my heart and life as my savior. Thank You for salvation. Forgive me of my past and present sins. You are my Father, protector and healer. I believe in you and Thank You for your amazing grace and mercy. Thank You for your unconditional love. For in Jesus name we pray. AMEN!

I now will pray for you that are hurting. Dear Father, I know you perform miracles in our lives today. You have performed miracles in my life. I Thank You! I pray for people that are hurting. People that have addictions, disease, depression, low self-esteem, that you will heal them. Father I know you can take away these hurts and we can hold our heads high because you are in us and never would leave us or forsake us. I thank you for your future blessings and for these people by accepting Jesus as their Savior they can cast away their illnesses, worries, anxieties and thoughts of suicide. AMEN!

My favorite prayer!

Matthew 6:9 (King James Version) Our Father who art in heaven. Hallowed be your name. Thy kingdom come, thy will be done on Earth as it is in Heaven.

Give us this day our daily bread and forgive us our trespasses as we forgive those who trespass against us. Lead us not in temptation but deliver us from evil. For thine is the kingdom, the power and glory forever. AMEN!

"VERSES"

Philippians 4:13 (NJKV version)

I can do all things through Christ who strengthens me.

Deuteronomy 31:8 (NIV version)

The Lord himself goes before you and will be with you; he will never leave you nor forsake you. Do not be afraid; do not be discouraged.

GOD BLESS YOU!

Journal

Date: _____

Journal

Date: _____

CONCLUSION

"TRAPPED"

Don't be trapped into thinking there is no one to turn to or you are not worth it. You are valuable to God. God has a purpose and a plan for your life. He loves you. He cries when he sees you hurt and broken.

Don't be consumed with making other people wanting to accept you. Be yourself and accept who you are. God made us each special and unique. He created each and every one of us. Each one of us has his own fingerprint. Wherever you are in your life at this moment I want to encourage you there is hope. You can change your circumstance. There are programs out there that can help you.

I encourage you to get in a Christian program. A church that teaches the bible. Find a doctor that you can trust. Do the research, and don't be afraid to ask questions. Expect to be treated with professionalism. But more importantly don't be afraid to have a relationship with Jesus. We have a father in heaven that loves us unconditionally. Seek and you will find, knock and the door will be open and pray and your prayers will be answered said the Lord.

"A NEW BEGINNING"

For More Information

Many thanks to Debbie Hutchinson.

You can visit her blog at

www.DrHutchBlog.com

Love you, Debbie!

Journal

Date: _____

_____
_____
_____
_____
_____
_____
_____
_____
_____
_____
_____
_____
_____
_____
_____
_____
_____
_____
_____
_____

Journal

Date: _____

_____
_____
_____
_____
_____
_____
_____
_____
_____
_____
_____
_____
_____
_____
_____
_____
_____
_____

Journal

Date: _____

_____
_____
_____
_____
_____
_____
_____
_____
_____
_____
_____
_____
_____
_____
_____
_____
_____
_____
_____
_____

Journal

Date: _____

_____
_____
_____
_____
_____
_____
_____
_____
_____
_____
_____
_____
_____
_____
_____
_____
_____
_____
_____
_____
_____

Journal

Date: _____

Journal

Date: _____

_____
_____
_____
_____
_____
_____
_____
_____
_____
_____
_____
_____
_____
_____
_____
_____
_____
_____

Journal

Date: _____

_____
_____
_____
_____
_____
_____
_____
_____
_____
_____
_____
_____
_____
_____
_____
_____
_____
_____
_____
_____

Journal

Date: _____

Journal

Date: _____

Journal

Date: _____

Journal

Date: _____

_____
_____
_____
_____
_____
_____
_____
_____
_____
_____
_____
_____
_____
_____
_____
_____
_____
_____
_____

Journal

Date: _____

_____
_____
_____
_____
_____
_____
_____
_____
_____
_____
_____
_____
_____
_____
_____
_____
_____
_____
_____
_____
_____
_____

Journal

Date: _____

Journal

Date: _____

_____
_____
_____
_____
_____
_____
_____
_____
_____
_____
_____
_____
_____
_____
_____
_____
_____
_____

ABOUT THE AUTHOR

This book is dedicated to my Mother who died January 4, 2008. That is when I started writing.

In my childhood I did have two parents with schizophrenia. Depression and addiction were major issues in our household. I encourage you to order a copy of this book for someone you know who is struggling or pass your copy on to someone with these life situations.

My story brings hope, healing, and salvation. I pray you will take my principles and learn to live a life of peace, joy and happiness with Jesus Christ. I have been on both sides of the track and the best is with Jesus. We are all in this together.

God Loves You and I Love You.

Made in the USA
Charleston, SC
19 August 2015